CHANDRA ZIEGLER

THE PHOENIX WITHIN

DREAM STAR DRAGONFLY

THE PHOENIX WITHIN

BY CHANDRA ZIEGLER

Extraordinary Endurance
Let Nature Be Your Teacher
The Phoenix Within

COPYRIGHT

Address all inquiries to:
Chandra Ziegler

chandraziegler@gmail.com

www.DreamStarDragonfly.com

ISBN: 979-8-9852600-2-1

Editors: S. Wonfor, C. Ziegler

Cover Design: Melanie Bess The Swimming Owl

Interior Design: Chandra Ziegler

Every effort has been made to properly source all quotes.

DEDICATION

To all the teachers of the world...with your hands full of white board marker smudges, your hearts full of trauma and unconditional love, your heavy minds full of stories...you are heroes beyond comparison. I see you. I hear you. I feel you. I honor you. Thank you for your dedication to education. You are an inspiration.

With love and gratitude,

Chandra

CONTENTS

CONTENTS

CHAPTER

1

INTRODUCTION

In my first book, *Extraordinary Endurance: A Training Plan for the Marathon of Life*, I write, "You know what got me to that finish line? You could call it stubborn determination or something else. I call it love."

I wrote that "Love has extraordinary power, extraordinary healing, extraordinary everything."

While I believed it to a degree, it wasn't until I faced some pretty heavy personal, professional, and marital challenges and came out on the other side glowing and full of grace that I truly understood the meaning of the phrase.

Finding the right title for a book is a bit like naming a child. I could have named this baby Extraordinary Love, as a sequel of sorts to my first. After much reflection, I eventually settled on *The*

Phoenix Within because it wasn't until I reached a deep dark place that I was able to burn it all and begin again.

The mythical bird reminds us all of the inner light we carry and inspires us to do what it takes to keep the flame alive.

This book pretty much wrote itself. I basically documented many of the shitty things that happened in my life as a teacher, in my marriage, and around the country during the global pandemic. When things started to settle I kept coming back to these pages as a way to make sense of everything that had transpired.

It's poetic and painful. Real and unrefined. It's a love story that could've gone awry. It's a peek into the lives of educators and human beings, hurting and hoping during one of the most traumatic periods in history.

My amazing partner and I held each other as we separately, yet collectively walked through our own valleys, one that I attempted to record here, the other that would follow suit shortly after. Peaks and valleys. Peaks and valleys. I think I have finally found peace in the rhythm.

I didn't want to publish this book. It felt too vulnerable. I often asked myself, what do I have to gain from sharing this with the world? This is too personal. Am I going to hurt someone? Who else would want to hear my story? I don't know those answers, but I know what happens if you let those negative voices stop you from fulfilling your dreams...nothing!

There is power in the written word and even greater power in the revealing of hidden truths. Honestly, there is more to the story than I share within these pages. For now, this was as far as I could go. I hope and I pray that there are pages that you dogear, phrases that you underline, words that speak to your soul. This is me. And now, I will turn it over to you.

Whether you're reading this in the year 2023 or 2123, I hope this book is a comfort to you, dear reader. May it remind you that it's okay to be exactly where you're at, it's okay to let people know how you really are and ask for help if you need it. It's okay to express your wants and needs, your greatest fears and deepest desires. It's okay to admit when you're wrong; to ask for forgiveness and more importantly, allow yourself to be forgiven.

I hope this book will inspire you to send a thank you note to a teacher. If you are a teacher, I hope you realize your worth and know that if you taught through the pandemic, you can do anything. Most importantly, I hope by reading this you will be one step closer to seeing your truest smile return to your beautiful face.

May you find the phoenix within!

FROM CLARITY TO CLUSTERFUCK

_____

*"Insight enables you to know your own heart.
Clarity enables you to accept without illusion."*

- Deepak Chopra

January 1, 2020

2020
A year of seeing clearly
Clear mind
Clear vision
If only we could envision
what the year had in store

Stories so unclear
Minds hurting
Vision blurred

As we were to stare helplessly
at the death toll rising
Along with our fear, anxiety,
anger, resentment

Would the year leave us bitter
Or better?

Would we build our wings
as we fell
Or stay in
the burning pits of hell?

This story is mine to tell
And ours to bid farewell

To remember
So we never forget

January 20, 2020

The Center for Disease Control
confirms the first U.S.
laboratory-confirmed
case of COVID-19
in the U.S.

February 1, 2020

"Where is your soul?"
-Middle child

February 24, 2020

Energy class
Air dragon visited me
What is your message?
What is it you have to illuminate?
What must we all rise above?

Trust your inner voice.
Let your spiritual knowledge
guide you.
Speak the truth of your soul
for all to hear.

The spirit world
was trying to warn us

Trying to guide me

March 9, 2020

Dear Teachers,
We're carrying on
business as usual

So was told to all
at parent teacher conferences

Teachers sat side by side
At our traditional
potluck dinner
Our last supper

How were we to know
That no,
business would never
be usual again

How was I to know
That the virus would spread
like wildfire
through the crevasses
of my mind and heart

March 10, 2020

A huge snake visited me
in my dreams

It tried to bite me

I threw a hurdle in its mouth
just in time
Another divine message
from the spirit world

A bite is coming

March 13, 2020

Friday the 13th
Beware the Ides of March
Ay, school is to be shut down
Goodbyes there were not
Everything canceled

April 5, 2020

Dear COVID-19
You shut down the schools
You shut down the parks
You shut down non-essential businesses
Now they're left in the dark

You shut down the churches
You shut down the malls
You shut down sporting events
Now we're left with phone calls

The things you've shut down
Keep piling up high
Spring break trips, movie theaters
Classes, lessons, clubs...bye bye

You've caused borders to close
And curfews to be set
We remain six feet apart
Or even further yet

You've caused so many deaths
Globally over 64 K
That number is rising
Each and every day

People are wearing gloves
And masks on their faces
Sadness and worry can be found
In so many places

I am writing to tell you
We will choose a different road
We will choose love and light
And lessen our load

We will open our minds
And let go of our fears
We will sit and meditate
And let our vision be clear

We will open up our hearts
And let love grow
We will show compassion
And reap what we sow

We will open up to the divine
That is in and around us all
From the stars and the rainbows
To the green sprout so small

You bring to us an awareness
Of a greater power at play
We surrender to that truth
And humbly go about our day

So we read and we write
And we notice a bit more
The beauty of a sunrise
Even more than before

We give thanks for cleaner water
Less congestion and clear air
We give thanks for our health
And the time we have to share

We can feel the Earth healing
And we know we're healing too
Of all the things we'd like to say
We choose, thank you

April 11, 2020

US Reports
highest daily death toll
amid COVID 19 pandemic
about 2,100 people died
on Friday

Confirmed cases of the coronavirus
have been reported
in nearly every country
around the world

US death toll is 18,778
Global death toll is 101,909

April 23, 2020

"When you're lonely,
just give your mom a hug
and call someone."
-Middle child

Our hearts break for all the moms lost
All the motherless children
All the hugs unable to be given
Our arms wrap tighter
Around the loved ones that remain
Reminding ourselves of the blessing
Of today
Of breath
Of health
Of heart

April 25, 2020

Spring is a time of renewal
Renewing a tattered,
downtrodden soul
Will hope spring eternal
During this uncertain time
This socially isolated time
This historical time?
Will we be eternally changed?
Evolve for the better?
A collective evolution
A Revolution

May 16, 2020

The sound of the spring peepers
is music to the ears
Notes of gratitude
small blissful moments

Momentary
Momentous

5:00 am fog under a rising sun
The rich smell of percolating coffee
Uninterrupted time to write
The first sleepy snuggles
with a messy piggy-tailed 2 year old
The joy in watching children be children
The kind words and hugs from a loved one

They are pure gold these day

May 19, 2020

You are allowed to dream big dreams.
You are allowed to not have any dreams.
You are allowed to try new things
and make mistakes.
You are allowed to be brave and bold
and reserved and timid at the same time.
You are allowed to wear dresses
and running shorts.
You are allowed to like rock and roll music
and dance like a ballerina.
You are allowed to play pretend
for as long as your heart desires.
You are allowed to do whatever
makes you happy and not fit the mold.
You are allowed to cry and yell and scream
and get angry at the world and the coronavirus.
You are allowed to feel all the feels
and not feel in control.
You are allowed to smile
even though you're sad
about all the human suffering.
You are allowed to be a light
and spread joy endlessly.
You are allowed to let your light flicker
in moments of despair
and let others do the heavy lifting.
You are allowed

June 5, 2020

Another innocent black man was killed
A police officer kneeled on his neck
for over 8 minutes
As he pleaded for his life

George Floyd, rest in peace

There will be justice
Peace there will be

We will remember your name
All the names
all the souls
Who have laid down their life
In this ongoing fight
Protests erupt around the world
Demanding justice,
a continued cry for change

An unpresidential president
added fuel to the fire
calling those who chose
to raise their voices
thugs and worse

These troubling, disturbing,
divisive displays of power
Will come to an end
And then

We shall overcome
We shall come together
We shall rise from the ashes
of our collective grief

June 6, 2020

COVID 19
cases in the US: 1,851,368
deaths: 107,172

COVID 19
cases in the world: 6,509,003
deaths: 385,770

June 7, 2020

"You okay mommy?"
-3 year old daughter

June 9, 2020

The ABCs of Teaching Social Justice

Acknowledge injustice
Build bridges
Choose kind
Demand change
Encourage conversations
Forgive others
Grow courageously
Have hope
Involve youth
Judge no one
Kick fear to the curb
Listen mindfully
Mend the wounds
Never give up
Open your heart
Practice what you preach
Question unfair rules and laws
Read critically
Spread love
Take action
Unite peacefully
Volunteer your time
Watch your words
X-ercise your right to vote
Yell when necessary
Zap out racism

EXHAUSTION

"Who has a book of all that monarchs do,
He's more secure to keep it shut than shown;
For vice repeated is like the wand'ring wind,
Blows dust in others' eye, to spread itself;
And yet the end of all is bought thus dear,
The breath is gone, and the sore eyes see clear
To stop the air would hurt them."

-William Shakespeare

July 7, 2020

"Are you okay?"
-retired teacher friend

July 28, 2020

Am I okay?
The truth is
I am drowning in devastation
The news is making me sick
Sick and tired
From lack of action,
lack of common sense,
Lackluster leadership at best
How are we to go back to normal
Back to in person learning
Amidst a raging pandemic
How are we to safely meet
the needs of those
entrusted to our care?
I. am. Not. okay. With. this.

July 29, 2020

My mind is troubled
Riddled with anxiety
The stress is eating me alive

Speaking up, speaking out
Speaking for those whose voices
have been extinguished
or would rather not
stick their neck out
has taken its toll

Navigating uncharted waters
of epic wildfire proportions
makes me want to roll into a ball,
curl up in the safety of a cocoon
But this I cannot
I will not

Human minds are sick
Detached from the natural world
The loss of respect for wild animals
and wild spaces,
greed,
and unbelievable short sightedness
led to this pandemic

But oh, what can I do
I feel so helpless
We must come together
We must rediscover our place
in the delicate web of life
But
first
we
must
survive

July 30, 2020

Do not give up on your beliefs
Stand strong and firm
Raise a gentle voice
Do what you must for the greater good

Thank you Spirit
I will persist

August 2, 2020

You say smile more
Be happier
Be a little kinder
Get rid of the cloud
Stop overreacting
Just be calm

Are you kidding me?
Life just has me a little weighed down

From trying to be a
strong,
kind,
positive role model
for our three young children,
quarantining for the past 5 months,
being separated from family and friends,
worrying about what is "right" or
"best" for our families health
and then feeling judged
based on those decisions,

Trying to show you how truly
unbelievably happy and proud I am of you
finally in the role that you've worked
so damn hard for and are amazing at
while simultaneously living
through a year from hell,

all the divisiveness,
unrest,
and political BS in our country,
the burden of having to make
life or death decisions
for an entire community,
all of it
I'm just tired

I don't need you to tell me to be more positive
That's not helpful
I need you to tell me
you understand ALL my feelings
and support me
I need you to tell me
it's okay to not be okay right now
I need you to tell me
you're there for me always
I need you to ask me
what you can do to help
I need you to hold me
in a comforting compassionate hug
when you don't know what else to say
I need you to give me
some grace and space
as I do the hard work
of returning to my inner peace

The cloud will eventually lift
I will smile more
I will find my calm and move on
We will weather this storm
and come out a bit more polished
in the end

August 6, 2020

"You like my dad so much.
My dad likes you so much."
-3 year old daughter

Oh how blinded by life
and the day to day grind we would become.
Little did we know how the year would
Test us
Tear us
Wear us down
Down we would not stay
Could not stay

August 7, 2020

Hugged my mom
for the first time
in eight months

Tears flowed like Niagara

August 24, 2020

Yo, Miss Ziegler, kick it one time girl
Yo, 2020, let's kick it
Coronavirus baby
Coronavirus baby

Alright stop
Sanitize and listen
Zig is back with this brand new edition

Someone grabs ahold of me tightly
Please take your seat don't touch me alrighty

Will it ever stop, yo, I don't know
Turn off the news and I'll show

To the extreme I rock a mask like a villain
Light up my room
And kids minds I'll be fillin

Read, in person or on Zoom
I'm fillin your brain
Virtually or in the classroom

Guessin, when I teach a dope lesson
Anything less than the best
You should question

Fever and coughin
You better stay back
You better get well, I'll keep you on track

If there is a problem, yo, we'll solve it
Check out the hook while
Miss Zig revolves it

Coronavirus baby
Coronavirus baby
Coronavirus baby
Coronavirus baby

Now that the school year is jumpin
With precautions kicked in
And sanitizer pumpin

Quick to your room
To your room no fakin
I'm cookin up math
Like a pound of bacon

Assessin you so I can help you please
I go crazy when I hear a sneeze

So I back up, behind my plexiglass yo
I'm on a roll, it's time to go solo

Rollin, in my classroom yo
With my windows open
So the air can blow

The Zoomers on standby
E-learning is so fly
Will you stop?
No, or I might cry

Kept on, inspiring and I won't stop
Busted my tail
And I'm heading to the next block

The kids were gone yo,
So I continued to A1A
Quarantine Avenue

Teachers were home in virtual meetings
Doing their best
With their temperatures heating

Worried, cause they can't give you a hug
Shay with the COVID
And Vanilla with a bug

Ready, for the year to begin
Gotta stay flexible so we can win

School clocks, rang out like a bell
I grabbed my mask so I can stay well

Walkin, in the hallways real fast
Stop at your locker
Get going to your next class

Hour to hour my minds getting packed
What do I do now
My computer got hacked

Tech support on the scene
You know what I mean
They passed me up
Confronted all the dope teens

If there is a problem, yo, we'll solve it
Check out the hook while
Miss Zig revolves it

Coronavirus baby
Coronavirus baby
Coronavirus baby
Coronavirus baby

Take heed cuz I'm a teacher poet
FPs on the scene
In case you didn't know it

My class will break the ceiling of glass
With plenty of kindness
And just enough sass

Cuz the hearts I've just gotta fill
With love and knowledge
I can never sit still

Public education
Is a heck of a concept
We make it hype
And you want to step with this

Whatever your grade
Take care of yourself
Don't let your spirit fade

So cool, other teachers say woah
If my lessons were prescriptions
I'd be makin lots of dough

Keep my composure in an election year
Magnetized by love
And never by fear

If there is a problem, yo, we'll solve it
Check out the hook while
Miss Zig revolves it

Coronavirus baby
Coronavirus baby
Coronavirus baby
Coronavirus baby

Yo, let's start the school year
Word to your mother

Coronavirus Baby Ah Choo, Ah Choo
Coronavirus Baby Ah Choo, Ah Choo
Coronavirus Baby Ah Choo, Ah Choo
Coronavirus Baby Ah Choo, Ah Choo

September 2, 2020

I interrupt your news feed
with a glimpse
into the inner workings
of a teacher's classroom
and mind during a global pandemic

19 face to face kids,
spread out as far apart as possible,
in many cases not far enough
all facing front,
wearing masks,
dehydrated, desensitized, depressed

5 virtual kids
sitting safely at home
All facing their own screens
and virtual realities
Unmasked
Unable to learn with their class
Zoom in, zoom out

sanitizing hands, desks,
and shared supplies
so often it makes me dizzy
screening for COVID symptoms

preparing emergency sub plans
for the inevitable
going above and beyond in so many ways

being stretched to oblivion
Doing two full time jobs at once
with no extra pay,
no extra praise

Learning new ways
of teaching
Teaching equity, responsibility,
resiliency, kindness

Trying not to compare oneself
to others who seem
to have it all together
This is a falsity

Taking in the news and numbers
COVID deaths
Deaths from racial injustice
Deaths by suicide

Parents barging through locked doors
Posing threats
Claiming I'm using "devil worship"
"violating civil rights"
They won't stop their emboldened,
misinformed, bullying
Until I stop what I'm doing
and mindfulness
is eradicated from the school

What the fuck kind of world are we living in?

This is the new reality we teachers face,
for those that try to go above and beyond
for the well being of their students,
for those with experience and wisdom
and compassion
to the nth degree,
for those who speak out,
we're punished and pummeled
with verbal assaults
Even though we willingly
put our lives on the line
just by being present
Oh how easily it is to forget the fact
that we would protect your children
from incoming bullets

Rallying the troops,
the keepers of light,
the wise ones
Defending my use of research-based
mindful approaches to teaching and learning
Praying for strength
to make it through this year

I am exhausted
It's only day 5
Help me
Please,
for the love of God

September 25, 2020

As the trees prepare for a deep slumber
Their colors intensify
I wonder why
They seem to be most brilliant
Before their most quiet of days
They unabashedly show their true colors
And then they shed
what no longer serves them

So it is with my spirit these days
The deep complex hues within
Have risen to the surface
Painting purpose for the world to see

When the time comes
And the north wind blows
I will give one final shake
and leave my spirit leaves behind

For what is mine is yours
No longer part of me
But of the Earth
Giving nourishment for new life
Space for regeneration
Time for growth

I breathe in the beauty
and mystery of the season
I breathe out my worries
And let them go
with the winds of change

I raise my hands to the sky
And offer my eternal gratitude
I return to my heart
Close my eyes
Wrapped in extraordinary peace

October 1, 2020

sorry, you can't hug your friends,
sorry we can't visit grandma and grandpa,
sorry you can't have a friend birthday party,
sorry you can't do parkour,
sorry you can't go trick or treating
I'm just sorry,
really really sorry

October 20, 2020

School was shut down for two weeks
Health department recommended
it remain shut down
for an additional two weeks
School board voted against
the recommendations -
the science, the facts, the professionals
and decided to reopen school

I used my hard earned sick days
to check off some medical appointments
and focus on my shriveling mental health
while trying to help with our daughters'
virtual learning
I was told by school officials
that I would not be allowed
to use my sick days

I fought it
I stood strong in my beliefs
I cried
I was ready to quit
I was supported by a few
I was disappointed
by the silence of many
I was reminded of my why
I was stripped from my pay
I received a handwritten note
excusing me from work from my doctor

My days/pay were reinstated

I might radiate positivity and wear
rose colored glasses
but don't fuck with me
like,
ever

.

October 21, 2020

Nothing about this year has been easy.
It has tested us in countless ugly ways.

Teachers have fought and fumbled.
We have tried to never let fear stop us
from doing and saying the right thing.
Most importantly,
by the grace of God,
we have faced each new day
with strength and love.

We don't need a cheerleader.
We don't want people to tell us
to just suck it up and do our job.

We need someone
to rest their hand on our backs
and let us know without saying a thing
it's okay not to be okay.
We need leaders
who are willing and able
to make tough decisions
with the health of all in mind

and possibly even willing
to take over our class
for a period of time.

Life is just a lot right now.
We're fighting continuous uphill battles.
We're all feeling it in different ways.

We're in the midst of a cosmic transformation
with work going on at all levels.
Humankind as a whole is figuring out
how to be
human
and
kind
at the same time.

October 27, 2020

Sweet 9 year old daughter of mine:
"I don't want love in five minutes,
I want love right now!"
"I hope this mandala
will bring peace to the world."
"I want to use my voice."

Sweet 6 year old daughter of mine:
"You're making me have tears."
"I see an angel."
"You're the strongest mom ever."

Sweet 3 year old daughter of mine:
"Open the damn door!"
"Christmas is closed. Santa is closed."
"I am not giving up."

November 7, 2020

11:30 am
Crows caw caw cawing
Soaring joyfully, circling, spreading the news
Joe Biden and Kamala Harris
won the presidential election
We joined the cacophony
with our own ear piercing
screams and shouts
And ran countless victory laps
barefoot around the house

"While I may be the first woman in this office,
I will not be the last,
because every little girl
watching tonight
sees that this
is a country of possibilities."
-Kamala Harris

The page has turned
A new chapter is being written
Let it be called Love, unity, truth, and justice
for ALL

November 20, 2020

"Congratulations Mrs. Ziegler,
you've been selected
as one of Michigan's
most resilient teachers."

re·sil·ient
/rəˈzilyənt/
adjective
1. (of a person or animal) able to
withstand or recover quickly
from difficult conditions.

Oh the irony
Teaching resilience
Exuding resilience
Feeling everything but
Resilient

Appearance and actions
Can mask the truth

Does simply surviving make one resilient?
How are we to recover quickly
from such difficulties
Such pain
Such trauma?

This trophy of resilience
belongs to educators everywhere
Those who continue to
Wake up
Rise up
Cape up
Mask up

Yet still we wait for help
As we cry for someone
Anyone
To hear our worries
Relieve our strain
Give us support and supplies
Appreciate our collective worth

December 1, 2020

The steam is gone
I have no energy left
I am tired
No,
I am exhausted
The fatigue (and compounded guilt)
I feel as a teacher
is incomparable

I'm supposed to love what I do
and do everything with a smile
because I love the kids I teach.
Truly, they are my why,
the sole reason I return day after day
through this global pandemic.

Yet still the truth remains,
I am tired of showing up to work
in an environment that puts me at risk
for contracting COVID 19.
I am tired of people
not taking this virus seriously
and treating me like a pawn in a chess match.
I am tired of people not doing MORE
to protect each other.
I am tired of people lying
and being selfish
and coming to school when they shouldn't.

I am tired of asking my students
every mask related question you can think of
and tired of doing it in a kind way.
I am tired of sanitizing desks,
doorknobs,
and my hands until they bleed.

I am tired of trying to do two jobs at once.
No, I take that back...
I'm tired of being ALL the following
at the same time all day long...
a 3 ring circus leader, nurse, counselor,
actress, youtuber, motivational speaker,
custodian, therapist, psychologist,
yoga instructor, artist, and xyz.

I am tired of this new math curriculum.
I am tired of whining.
I am tired of kids not listening.
I am tired of smiling
and pretending everything is okay.
It's not.
I am tired of going above and beyond for others
(God that sounds so selfish).

I just need a break.
I had 30 minutes to myself today
and instead of using it to go for a run
or read a book
or make a good dinner
or ya know, have sex,

I went to school
and recorded a math video
for my virtual students...
which I will probably play
for my in person kids as well
because I'm so GD tired of everything.
Everything.

I feel so awful saying all these things.
I should be feeling thankful for my job,
thankful for my health,
thankful for all my blessings.
I am.
And I know I am incredibly privileged
to have all that I have
and be able to whine
about my exhaustion in the first place.

But I also have a right to share my truths.
We all do.
If I don't write them down,
I will explode.
I will literally self-combust.

December 5, 2020

The other night I cried myself to sleep
because I once again felt like a horrible mother
I gave and I gave and I gave
and I worked and I worked and I worked
all day long
Long after the clock said I could go home
I had a million things to do
and I wasn't present for my own children

All their questions and concerns
had to be hushed or brushed aside because
I was too busy checking in with virtual kids,
making videos to post for the next day,
looking over papers,
planning and organizing
to stay afloat for one more day

and I couldn't
I just couldn't

On the ride home with 3 kids yelling,
the panic set in
my already worn out patience
was blown to smithereens
I blew up at them
I just needed one second to breathe
and I never got it

I feel like I've been thrown onto a treadmill
going top speed
I feel like I'm treading water
and barely keeping my nose above the surface
I feel like I'm suffocating slightly,
with the unbearable pressure and expectations
I feel like a pawn in society's educational
coronavirus experiment
I just feel exhausted
I feel like I'm repeating myself to oblivion

December 7, 2020

"I don't want 2020 to end."
-oldest daughter

December 8, 2020

In the book
What A Wonderful Word:
A Collection of untranslatable words
from around the world
by Nicola Edwards and Luisa Uribe

We learn about this most perfect word

Ishq

It is Arabic for
"A perfect love without jealousy
or inconsistency
that holds two people together."

Is Ishq sold in a bottle?
Ours seems to be running out.

December 10, 2020

Gratitude journal entry:

"I'm alive."

December 21, 2020

It is in the darkest of dark
that the stars and moon
shine the brightest

It is in the dark nights
that the prayerful curls
of campfire smoke
can reach the heavens

It is in the cold dark skies
that the northern lights
shimmer their magical waves
of energy

Darkness is a given
It is beautiful and a gift
The dark allows us
to truly appreciate the light

I pray that the dark days
so many are living in right now
will be obliterated
by an even greater number of days
of light ahead

Or even better
I pray that the compacted darkness
will be a catalyst for cosmic growth
Fuel so strong and intense
to cause an explosion
of extraordinary love

I beg and plead that my cries
are heard, seen, answered
(hey God, they're the ones sent up
in technicolor sage-smelling smoke
through the flapping tattered shreds
of my prayer flags...
would it help if I got new ones?)

I remain hopeful
We must all remain hopeful
Light is coming
Even if it doesn't feel like it
It will come

December 28, 2020

Christmas was canceled
We took a day trip to be with family
Outdoors
On the coldest day of the winter

"Can I hug you grandma?"
- 3 year old daughter

A pause

Then tears

The ghosts of this panic of a pandemic
Will remain burned
in the psyche of humankind
For eternity

December 31, 2020

This year has been,
let's just say,
A lot

A lot of change
A lot of challenge
A lot of isolation
A lot of friction
A lot of mourning
A lot of staying home
A lot of uncertainty
A lot of shedding
A lot of growth

CHAPTER

4

SOMETHING'S GOTTA GIVE

---

*"To have and to hold,
from this day forward,
for better, for worse,
for richer, for poorer,
in sickness and in health
until death do you part."*

-A Nuptial Blessing

January 6, 2021

An angry mob of Trump supporters
stormed the nation's capitol
with the goal
of overturning the election
and stopping
the peaceful transfer of power.

The scene played over and over
in homes around the world
Showing the most
disgusting,
disrespectful
display of humanity

An evil power lived there
for hours - longer really

People were killed

We will never
be the same

To my teacher friends
who feel like they want
or NEED to do more
Who feel like they
can't go back to teaching
"regular school"

I encourage you to pause
reflect
consider the powerful role
you have to play

You can do more
We all must do more
Teach tolerance
Peaceful problem solving
The fucking golden rule

We can't morally teach
any other way

And
AND

Continue to vote
for stable people
who have the well being
of ALL in mind,
not just their own pocket book,
or the unborn,
or those who look
and sound like themselves,
or believe in the same higher power,
or love the same people

January 7, 2021

Dear COVID 19,
You kept us apart
You kept us without
You killed over 1 million people
You filled us with decay,
darkness, and doubt

White supremacy and violence
Reared their ugly heads
A disease of hatred and intolerance
Led even more to their deathbeds

We opened the churches
We opened the schools
We opened the businesses
With unfollowed rules

A vaccine was created
To bring an end to
your destruction
While others planned attacks
That led to
a shameful insurrection

After months of disruption
Confusion and dismay
Many people thought
You would just go away

CHANDRA ZIEGLER

So they took off their masks
And turned blind eyes
As the number of
human lives lost
Continued to rise

Some pointed fingers
Bullied others
and placed blame
Some rose above it all
The lives lost ticked
on just the same

You kept on mutating
and spreading
At an alarming rate
You tried to pull us apart
But humankind,
we choose our own fate

So as you continue to rage
To take lives and separate
We will fight against
the disconnect
For love and healing
we are desperate

We're still grappling
with numbers
Wandering in the dark of night
You cannot take our hope
We will be the light

January 17, 2021

When my heart is burdened
by intolerance,
injustice,
incompetence,
incomprehensible hate,
fear, bigotry,
violence, and silence

When my whole body
aches for justice,
peace,
mercy,
grace,
kindness,
understanding,
compassion,
unity,
and love

When my head
just wants to scream
and feels like
it's going to explode
with so many questions

What are you afraid of?
Why do you choose
to attach your identity
to a racist flag
that flies out of fear?
Why are you so cruel
toward your fellow
brothers and sisters?
Why do you throw stones?
Why do you sew hate?
Why are you so irate?
Were you not taught
how to collaborate?
What is it that
you wish to illuminate?

When my spirit is exhausted
by all the division
and longs for change

I am reminded of
Dr. Martin Luther King Jr's words,

"Change does not roll in
on the wheels of inevitability,
but comes through
continuous struggle."

I honor the struggle
of all those that have
come before me
and who continue
to struggle to this day

I honor those
whose voices are silenced
or whose lives are deemed
less worthy

I honor those
who raise their own voices
to stand up
for what's right,
to condemn what is wrong,
to speak out
regardless of consequences

I know that it's the struggle
that makes change possible
But still I ask,

Why is it so hard
to find common ground?
Why is it easier for so many
to fight rather than forgive?
Why can't we just
take one deep breath
and think about our choices?

Why can't we pause
and look our neighbors
in the eye?
Why can't we have change
with a little less suffering?

Change is coming
I feel it in my bones
The struggle will be laid to rest
Humankind will live up
to its potential

It is our namesake

We will learn to be KIND
We will heal the past
by righting our wrongs
We will realize there are no sides
We are all one family
One human race
One love

January 20, 2021

Inauguration Day

"It smells like victory."
-2nd grader

Joe Biden was sworn in
as the 46th President
of the United States

Kamala Harris was sworn in
as the first African American,
Asian American,
and woman Vice President
of the United States

Glass shattered

Amanda Gorman
spoke as the nation's
first ever youth poet laureate

Her words like medicine
to a weary country
A heart broken,
bleary eyed,
weary world

Still in the horrific midst
of a viral onslaught
Shadowed days
of diseased hearts
and misguided deeds

Yet

We march on knowing
The pen is mightier
than the sword
For it is in the right combination
of syllable and word
That pain can be forgotten
and hope can be restored

And we're allowed
to dream again
Write our own future
One filled with
beautiful rhymes
Happy endings
and no crimes

With harmony
rather than dissonance
A call to action
rather than dangerous
passive indifference

So we continue
to brandish our quill
As we speak our truths
and bid evil farewell

Rise together,
hands stretched
towards the light,
Ready to embrace
A more peaceful race

And settle, settle, settle
our differences,
our frazzled nerves,
our racing hearts

So we march on
Holding onto hope
Holding onto love
Holding onto
the promise of
A new day
A new way
Anyway

February 4, 2021

Trudging knee deep in water
A force whispered

Turn around

Swept away with the current —---
Current events
Current reality
Currently floating
blissfully in a dream world
Heading towards a waterfall

We let ourselves fall
No end in sight
No more pushing
No more being pushed
We close our eyes
for a moment
Feeling the rush
of the air
against our masked
or unmasked faces

Wild hearts set free

Then the crash comes
Brought back
from another plane

Eyes opened
To the pride,
ignorance,
selfishness,
greed,
death,
decay

March 9, 2021

Breathe in.
Breathe out.
Breathe in.
Breathe out.
Breathe in.

"Shut UP!!!"
"Don't talk to me."
"Leave me alone!"
"I don't want to do that."

Breathe in.

Don't forget to schedule
your observation.
Don't forget your attendance.
You'll need to fill out
this 17 page long
referral form
to get student Y help.

Breathe in.

Your lesson plans now
have to look like this.
You will now need to record
your absences this way.

No,
in fact,
your sick time
is not
your personal business.

Breathe in.

"She called me sassy."
"He won't be my partner."
"This is SO interesting."
"That's just great."
"He just punched me in the balls!!!"

Breathe in.

Zoom call number 12.
No answer.
Shit,
I forgot to post
the assignment for math
on Seesaw
and there are 21 other children
coming through the door.

"I hope my dad doesn't yell at me
when I go home."

Breathe in.

Plan the lesson.

Rehearse the lesson.
Revise the lesson.
Record the lesson.
Plan another lesson.
Rehearse another lesson.
Revise another lesson.
Record another lesson.

Breathe in.
Breathe in.
Breathe in.

Figure out
what math is going
to look like
in 15 minutes.
Prep materials.
Don't forget
to send so and so to the office.
Forget
to send so and so to the office.
Go apologize.
Email parents.

Breathe in.

"I just want to make this claw."
"I don't feel like doing that."
"This is too hard."
"I need help."
"Mrs. Ziegler.

Mrs. Ziegler.
Mrs. Ziegler.
MRS. ZIEGLER!!!!"
"I was here first!"

Breathe in.

Lay on floor
during relaxation time
and actually close my eyes.

"Are you okay Mrs.Ziegler?"

"Yeah."

"I'm just breathing out."

June 7, 2021

The battle is over
We're left battered,
bruised,
betrayed
By a system that said
they had our backs

When in reality
When our backs
were up against a wall
Our voices wailing for help
Our lights barely flickering

We were told to be quiet
To keep our opinions
to ourselves
To keep calm
and teach on
To fill in for others,
step up
To tutor above and beyond
On and on and on
Empty promises
Empathy gone

Unbeknownst to most
We're left broken
on the battlefield

Chests cut open
Our bloody hearts
barely beating

Beating
Beating
Beat
Beat
Beat
B
B
B

———————

June 8, 2021

This past year and a half
was a gigantic,
never ending,
swirling,
all-encompassing,
shitshow
of epic proportions.

I didn't feel resilient.
I didn't stay
balanced enough,
breathe enough,
follow the light enough,
run enough,
return to
my yoga mat enough,
or lean on
my loved ones enough
like I said I was going to.

I didn't actually follow
the advice my dreams
were sending me
to stop pushing.

I didn't slow down
like the Universe
had been trying
to tell me to do.

I didn't channel
my jaguar birthday
spirit animal enough
and let go of my fears.

Instead, I found myself
with more and more on my plate.
I ended up carrying a ton of stress.
forced to do more with less
working multiple
full time jobs in a
semi-toxic environment.

If someone (including myself)
tells me to be the light
one more Goddamn time
I am going to lose my SHIT!

I wanted to quit every other day.
I cried more often than not.
I felt misunderstood

No, I'm not fucking depressed

under appreciated,
unsafe,
exhausted,
manipulated.

Quite unlike the me
that I knew.
No wonder I simply
wanted to close my eyes
and walk away.

I didn't want
to slowly process anything.
I didn't want to talk.
I didn't recognize myself.
I didn't ask for help.

That was all way too hard.

I had enough of feeling
like I was barely holding
my nose above water.
I had enough running on fumes.
I had enough politics,
enough being told
or made to feel
that I needed to
keep staying positive
and just do my job
because that's
what teachers do,

enough bullshit,
enough stress.

I was done.

Ready to move on.
I just wanted to escape.

June 10, 2021

I connected with
a ghost
from the past
and felt momentarily
alive and well.

Thankful
to be free
from all
that had been.

I smiled.
I laughed.
I remembered.

So this is what it's supposed to be like.

I made poor choices.
I could feel
hear
sense
my spirit self
trying to shake me,
Wake me up,
Yelling,

Who are you?
What are you doing?

Honestly,
I didn't know who I was,
what I was doing,
or why I was doing it.

I sure thought I did,
But I was hurting
And when you're hurt,
you do stupid stuff.

I didn't want to look back.
I didn't want to think
about the endless tears
from the past year.

I was lost in a
lonely,
deep,
dark,
Like
really
really
really
dark
quagmire
of questions and musings.

I wasn't thinking clearly.
All my teacher training
prepared me to put up
an amazingly convincing front

(or maybe not)
that all was fine.

Masked mouth
Masked eyes
Masked heart
Masked from reality

I thought
something was wrong
with my marriage.

Silence,
doubts,
fears
crept into the crevices
of my mind.

My heart was
aching
Breaking
Pleading
with Jesus
to take the wheel.

How could I possibly feel
so selfish, sad, and stressed out
Unable to receive
the life support I
desperately needed

Traumatized

June 11, 2021

I almost walked away.
From everything.

I wasn't ready to point the finger
at the Post Traumatic Stress Disorder
that I should have been
diagnosed with
after the chaotic year.

I know I'm not alone in this.
Teachers around the world
are carrying immense trauma.

It's real
and ugly
and hard
and painful
and
and
must I go on?

No oxygen masks in sight
Asphyxiated brains
barely functioning

I just needed to get away.
Get away from
all the death,
all the trauma,
all the drama,
all the stress.

Away from reality
for just a blip in time.

June 14, 2021

I needed something big
to pull me out of the darkness
I was drowning in

naturally,
I signed up
for my first ultramarathon

A 50 kilometer trail race
Single track
5,000 feet elevation gain

Yes,
this was precisely the thing
my body, mind, and spirit
needed to get me
through the mess I was in

The journey to the finish line
would leave me
completely transformed
and healed
from the inside out

feeling stronger,
more resilient,
ready to fly,
ready to return to my love - fully

and hopefully strong enough
to return to teaching for another year

To a true ultrarunner,
50km is nothing.
For me,
in that moment,
it was everything.

I drank up training miles
like a butterfly sipping up
sweet sweet nectar

Every step was medicine

July 7, 2021

Who am I?

I am a woman
of the wilderness,
born to be wild and free.

I am a woman
with a free spirit,
connected
to the collective universal spirit
who desires to be with someone
who connects deeply to that pulse.

I am a woman
who is done struggling
and pretending
and smiling
because I should
and is okay with being by herself.

I am a woman
who needs space yet closeness.
To be held but not squeezed.
To be understood
and treated with gentleness.

I am a sensual woman
who longs for someone
who lights her up inside

and makes her heart
do somersaults.

I am a woman
who longs to write
and share her visions
with the world.

I am a woman
who needs creative space
to make messes
because that's
where inspiration flourishes
and dreams unfurl.

I am a woman
with an adventurous soul
who longs to travel
and see the world
with a partner
who can't wait
to join in on the joy
of experiencing other cultures
and growing closer together.

I am a woman
who strives to embody
strength, courage, love,
honesty, worthiness,
kindness, sassiness,
wisdom, wildness,

humility, beauty,
and complete faith
in self and God.

I am a mother
who wishes
with all her heart and soul
to pass these virtues
onto her children.

I am a woman
who is trying desperately
to listen to her heart
and trust her intuition.

I am a woman
who needs more
laughter and joy in her life.

I am a woman
who needs to be released.

I am me.

Perfectly imperfect.
Beautiful and flawed.
Full of wonder
and just a touch of fear.
With a heart
that needs to fly.

July 10, 2021

You are going through
a powerful metamorphosis.
You need to release
and spread your wings.
Just stay patient and trust.

-Monarch Butterfly

July 21, 2021

Thank God for the therapists
Who intervene
Intercept a car
careening off a cliff
Internalize
worries and wounds
And share the wisdom
of darkness unseen

Thank the lucky stars,
the holy land,
the ancestral wisdom
That radiates intergalactically
At exactly the perfect time
beautiful trees
reach arms in an offering
giant rock outcroppings
of pure quartz
full of healing energy

energetic fields cleared
ancestors honored
spirits called in
words spoken and unspoken
tears
offerings

drum beat

bum bum bum bum
bum bum bum bum
bum bum bum bum

Journey

something moved
within and around

Release
Allow
Return

July 23, 2021

California
2 weeks away from reality
Just us

My husband and I
An escape

Will it make
or break
Will it heal
Or will we
continue to reel?

Two people
Too much pain carried
To do this alone

Come, spirits, come

July 25, 2021

Husband: You shouldn't be yelling
in a Zen house.

Wife: Why the hell not?
This is EXACTLY where
I should be shouting,
swearing, and releasing.
How can I return to my
Zen-like nature
without letting all the shit go?

July 26, 2021

The Pacific Coast air,
Japanese house,
and ancient furniture
Allowed us
to sit and stare
air our truths

Bare our souls
and our skin
Begin again

To forgive,
heal,
return
to one another

July 27, 2021

Dear sweet, salty ocean,
the ebbs and flows
of your water
moving in rhythm
with the moon
pull on my emotions so

the turquoise
blue green waves
that crash mightily
send ripples
of wind
through my hair

And oh
your breath heals
your salt sustains
You keep me afloat

Thank you
Thank you
Thank you

July 28, 2021

The Universe
has been working overtime

Call it what you may
Coincidence
Divine intervention
Miracles
God winks
However spoken,
the results
are still the same

Love conquers all

July 29, 2021

"The secret of marriage
is communication,
and a little fight
to keep things steamy!"

-Marco, Golden Eagle Resort,
Trinidad, CA

July 30, 2021

They are old and bold.
They are wise and never try
to be anything but themselves.
They are beautiful and twisted,
gnarly and gifted.
They are full of life,
receptors of
our collective joy and strife.

As I stood humbly before
another giant Redwood,
I was flooded with
a much deeper awareness
of these wise, resilient beings.
I stood there contemplating
how trees have such
extraordinary memories.

With my feet firmly planted,
I could feel vibrational messages
from my energetic being
traveling deep into the earth.

The intertwining roots
of all the trees around me
drank up those pulsing waves
along with life-giving water.

They were simultaneously
soaking in my carbon dioxide
as I breathed in their oxygen.
What a natural yet magical
and incredibly intimate relationship.

In that moment, I began to cry
because I realized how much
we needed each other.
I extended my shaking hand
and rested it on the tree's trunk
in an act of gratitude
and to seek forgiveness.
The tree has given so much
and has grounded me.

Softly,
I placed my forehead
on the gnarly trunk
and in that moment,
as if the tree read my mind,
the wind began to blow
gently through the branches
and the leaves whispered,

"My dear turtle dove,
I have known the longings
of your heart since
before you were born.
Your spirit has danced
around my limbs since
the beginning of time.

Your soul is limitless
and light embodied
and you long to fly.
Your song needs to be sung
for others to be set free.

I might be grounded here,
yes, my dear,
but every year
I let myself fly
and spread my seeds,
my soul,
far and wide.
It is natural,
these feelings you carry,
that seep through the soil
and soak into me.
It is natural and it is
the way forward.

Know that I am always here.
You can nest in my branches.
You can dance upon

the wind on my crown.
You can leave to soar
wherever your heart leads you
and trust that I
will always be here
when you return.
Know that you give me
as much as I give you.
Your breath, your energy
sustains me as mine does for you.

Truly you and I are leaves
of the same tree.
At times we will feel far apart.
This is natural too my love.
Just look down
to see where we have been.
Our roots reach deep.
Our truths entwined together.
Our branches stretch
in all directions
but our leaves face the same sun.
When you feel called,
release, return to source,
let go and allow yourself
to break free.
This is the rhythm of life.

Let me leave you with this...
you must let go
in order to find space
to reconnect with your true pulse.
You must sing your song
for the world to hear.
All of it.
All the mud.
All the magic.

You are a miracle my sweet turtle dove.
You bring happiness and light
wherever you go.
Thank you for sharing
that light with me."

As I opened my eyes
and caressed the twisted,
weathered trunk of the tree,
I looked down and gave thanks.
Then, I cast my gaze to the sky
where leaves were swaying
and I smiled,
knowing my spirit has been,
was then,
and will continue
to dance there,
with this special tree,
into eternity.
I paused and then spoke.

But dear tree spirit,
why is it so hard
to embody these truths
in real life?
Why does it feel
like such a struggle sometimes?
Why do I cry so much?
Why do I resist
being loved and taken care of?

Another gust of wind and then,

"My love,
those worries and fears
are all in your mind.
They are not yours to carry.
They do not belong to you.
They serve as distractions
in your transformation.
In order to continue to grow,
evolve,
dance,
sing,
live grounded,
yet fly free,
you must release those doubts,
those questions.
Stop resisting.
You can trust your soul and your intuition.
All you need to do is breathe in...
deep down into your roots

that live in Mother Earth.
She will support you.
Then breathe out...
and look up to Father Sky.
He will guide you.
It takes patience.
You are in no rush.

Know that everything you need
is already in you.
You are truly an enlightened being.
I will always be here
to guide you back onto the path.
When your emotions
get the better of you,
just smile and laugh
and return to your beating heart.
Emotions are momentary.
Love is eternal bliss.
Decide in those moments
to choose love.
Slow your breath.
Feel my branches cradling you.
See your spirit dancing
and all will be well.

Your life on Earth is temporary.
You,
my dear turtle dove,
are eternal.
That is why it's all so hard.

You struggle with not wanting
to miss a thing.
You know how short your human life is
and you don't want to waste a moment.
But you must trust that
every struggle,
every smile,
every song
is for your higher good,
for the collective evolution
of all your loved ones.
Choose love. Sing your song."

The whispers of the wind disappeared,
but the pulsing in my feet grew stronger.
I felt alive.
Refreshed.
Supported.
Understood.
Heard.
Wherever those words came from
is a Divine mystery.
Once again, I bowed my head
and surrendered to the ever powerful,
unwavering love of God
and support of the Universe.

July 31, 2021

If you would like to know
strength and courage,
welcome the company of trees.

Trees are alive in such
a powerful and mysterious way.
They know exactly
what we need to heal.

Trees are strong,
aren't afraid to be themselves,
aren't afraid of storms,
they have courage to grow deep,
stretch high,
and bend,
knowing they'll eventually break.

In California
With the wisest of the wise
I allowed myself to sit,
be still and silent,
surrender to
all the feelings and all the truths,
and receive a message
that flowed through my hand
as if it were an extension
of that living, breathing, wise tree.

We must allow ourselves
to be still to heal.

We must also
take action
to protect wild spaces.

In changing our relationship with
Mother Earth
and seeing ourselves
as an integral part of nature,
a part of the interconnectedness
of all living things,
we will not only heal
our relationship
with the planet
and right our wrongs,
but also heal our relationships
with each other.

Amen.

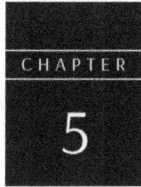

CHAPTER

5

LOVE IS VIRAL

---

*"Love is the whole thing.
We are only pieces."*

-Rumi

August 3, 2021

Love is ugly.

A fuck you, how could you kind of thing.
Why is it that those we love the most
often get treated the worst.
They get the joy of seeing us
ugly cry and act in childish ways.
But if not with our loved ones,
then with who?
Frankly, this is how it should be.
We should be allowed
to let down our guards at home.
If we hold it all in,
then the rest of the world
gets the ape-shit crazy,
rated R version of who we are.
It's certainly not
my favorite description of love.
But thank God love is big enough
to hold space for the ugliness.
And I thank my lucky stars
that I found someone
who will stay by my side
through the ugly periods.

Love is ugly.

Love is beautiful.

Aw, now that's more like it.
Love is a beautiful thing.
A wow, you look good
in a convertible thing.
A fresh flowers
in a vase thing.
A pumpkin at your
dorm room door kind of thing.
A snapshot of our smiles
frozen for eternity kind of thing.

Love is beautiful.

Love is a feeling.

Wild.
Electric.
Tingly.
Warm.
Vital.
An inner knowing.
Love gives you the feeling
that you can take on the world.
If you can't feel love,
what the hell's the point?
Y'all, people die
from broken hearts
all the time.

Love is a feeling.

Love is a decision.

This is the hardest one I think.
When we make the conscious decision
to continue to fight for our love
when all we want to do is give up.
When I'm annoyed as hell
at something
and choose to ignore it.
When I'm caught in a rabbit hole
and part of me
kind of wants to stay there
and explore a little longer,
I have to decide
to retreat and hop back
on the right path
with my own two feet.

Love is a decision.

Love is eternal.

It lasts forever.
Just like I know
our love is meant to be.

Love is eternal.

Love is chaos.

Girls singing
and shouting
and dancing
and wrestling.
Toys and books strewn everywhere.
Permanent marker and paint stains.
Dirty socks left on the counter.
Endless loads of laundry.
Bath time. Story time. Poop scoop time.
No, I want to snuggle with mommy time.
Cook the meal. Eat the meal.
Whine about the meal.
Clean up from the meal.
Repeat.
Plan the trip.
Pay the bills.
Get to this appointment.
Run here. Run there.

Love is chaos.

Love is bliss.

And then, the pause.
The quiet moments
where we lock eyes,
see each other's souls,
and recognize
the gift of the moment
and the life we've built together,
are pure bliss.

Slow dancing in the kitchen,
getting a shoulder rub,
watching and listening
to girls squeal
and giggle with delight
as you tackle and tickle them
is bliss eternal.

Holding hands with you
while walking along the ocean,
keeping our Great Lakes boat
on a semi straight path
towards the endless blue horizon,
skiing with you through
a diamond studded forest
is bliss embodied.

Laying on the ground
gazing up at the stars with you
somewhere in the wilderness,
how you make me feel like a Goddess
talk about beyond bliss.

The yes yes yes
feeling of pure ecstasy
that I finally
passionately allow myself to feel.

Love is bliss.

Love is fucking hard.

I hate arguing.
It triggers me.
I start to spiral.
It's hard to work through the tough stuff.
But when you have a love like we do,
you just do.

Love is fucking hard.

Love is God.

God is love.
You and I were created
in the image of God
so we ARE love embodied.
God is a part of us.

Love is God.

Love is viral.

Just as the coronavirus
crept, lept, and spread
like wildfire,
taking lives,
destroying homes,
leaving spirits frayed,
families in dismay,
communities reeling,
countries dealing
with hospital inundation,
pandora's box of misinformation,
scrambled system of education;
love acts
in extraordinarily similar ways.
Love spreads quicker,
circulates wider,
taking lives and pulling them
closer together,
preserving homes,
leaving spirits full,
families in delight,
communities healing,
countries feeling hopeful
despite the obstacles.
Thank God the viral effects of love
conquers all.

Love is viral.

Love is forgiveness.

There's nothing quite like
saying the words I'm sorry.
But then again,
there's nothing quite like
hearing the words I'm sorry.
MMM, that's love.
What's more
is the incredible truth
that despite all our failures and flaws,
poor choices and poorly selected words,
we are forgiven.
You are forgiven.
I am forgiven.
Because God's love is SO huge.
And that my friends
is the greatest gift.
It's not an easy out.
We still have to do the work
of forgiving others
and the even harder work
of forgiving ourselves.
But in the end, how amazing it is
that we can take a deep breath
and just rest in that expansive love.

Love is forgiveness.

Love is blind.

A let me feel your hand
fit perfectly in mine love.
An, ah yes,
that's my man's smell love.
A smile ear to ear
from your high pitched laughter love.
A hold me just right
everything will be okay love.
A conscious choice
to look past each other's imperfections
kind of love.

Love is blind.

Love is steady.

The Earth revolves steadily
around the sun
and the moon waxes and wanes,
each always returning
to the same position,
in a regular, completely natural cycle,
so too does our love.
After fifteen years of marriage,
I think you have finally picked up
on how in sync my moods are
with the changing of the moon.
You've learned not to take what I say
too personally around the full moon.
I'm hella charged
and full of energy
and passion
and fire
and spice.

You are definitely the steady to my samba.
Sometimes I wish you would just let loose
and salsa with me under the stars,
but I also appreciate the fullness of you.
I've come to realize and appreciate
all the different seasons
of change,
ups and downs,
storms and serenity
that come with marriage.
When we're in a valley,
I can look forward to another peak
or a relatively calm, flat period as well.

Love is steady.

Love is protection.

Like when I wanted to sign up
for my first marathon
after going through our second miscarriage
and life sucking surgery
and being so mad at my body
for betraying me
and wanting to say fuck you,
look what I can do,
and you said,
someday honey, but not now.

Running has always been
a natural form of healing.
I had a lot of healing to do,
but you were protecting me,
my recovering body,
and my broken traumatized heart.
You are my protector.
As I am yours.

Love is protection.

Love is complicated.

Like a giant onion.
It is layered and complex,
insanely beautiful,
with hidden truths
that will sometimes make you cry.

Love is complicated.

Love is messy.

A here darling,
let me wash your hair
and try to put it up in a messy bun
like you so effortlessly do
and I have never done before
because your collarbone is broken
and you can't move your arm
without piercing pain
shooting through your body
kind of love.
A clean up from the aftermath
of a projectile puke session
without the blink of an eye
kind of love.
A van layered with so much stuff
after a road trip to the Smoky Mountains
that an archeologist would die to dig in
and make epic discoveries
kind of love.

Love is messy.

Love is happenstance.

Did we truly just happen
to fall in love with each other because
we were on the same ski team
at the same time?
Or would we have found each other
regardless?
I told you early on in our love story
that our names were written together
in the stars
since the beginning of time
and we were meant for each other.
Boy I was head over heels
in love with you.
I'm not sure about a lot of things,
but I have faith in
a bigger power at play,
and I am sure about
the unwavering force of love.
Happenstance or not,
I love you still.
Somedays I feel like cartwheeling
head over heels with joy
because we get to spend forever together.

Somedays I feel myself tighten up
and just want to go to bed early.
But still, we're together
and we will let love happen
surely my stance will melt a bit
I'll return with renewed salt and vinegar
sugar and spice
and show up to tend to our love.

Love is happenstance.

Love is dark.

We have dealt with many dark days
and nights together.
There will inevitably be more to come.
It is in those moments
that we can truly appreciate
the light.
It is in that dark space
that other types of light,
other voices,
other signs
can shine through
and offer hope or an answer.

Love is dark.

Love is light.

This is the kind of love
that makes everything else worthwhile.
It's the smile and embrace
at the end of a long day.
It's diving headfirst
into a sparkling but freezing cold Lake Superior
and screaming at the top of our lungs.
It's a campfire blazing
and dancing in the breeze.
It's the glow of the logs in the sauna.
It's the flicker of a candle
on the dinner table.
It's the glow of the lamp in the bedroom
when all is finally quiet.

Love is light.

Love is like grapes.

Unique.
Bold.
Sweet.
Juicy.
Hot.
Requiring great amounts of light to grow.
And after being picked and smashed
and sent through the ringer,
and given enough time
to grow close together
and settle in the dark barrel of life,
will emerge even
stronger,
bolder,
and hotter than before
and leave you drunk on love.

Love is like grapes.

Love is ordinary.

A garbage in the garage,
groceries in the fridge,
laundry in the machine,
chili on the stove kind of love.
A pair of skis waxed and ready for race day,
no questions asked kind of love.

Love is ordinary.

Love is extraordinary.

All that love is
is exactly what makes it so extraordinary.
There is no one right description of love,
that's what makes it so -
perfect.
What makes our love extraordinary
is all the ordinary ways
we show up for each other.
It's also the surprises, the dates,
the "extravagant" things
(I say that with parentheses
because our idea of extravagance
is probably quite average
compared to others...
but hear me say, I am NOT
comparing our love...
that is the death of marriage).
Our love is extraordinary because
it's us.
Every day we're smiling and laughing
(sometimes swearing, but what the hell,
that's life and love)
and growing closer together.

I picture us all old and gray and wrinkly,
from all the ugliness and beauty,
all the feelings and decisions,
all the chaos and bliss,
all the hard complicated messes,
all the darkness and light,
shuffle skiing along in our spandex
and I smile the most genuine smile.
That's us.
We're in it for the long haul.
We know how to endure.

Love is extraordinary.

PHOENIX RISING

"Darkness cannot drive out darkness;
only light can do that.
Hate cannot drive out hate;
only love can do that."

-Martin Luther King, Jr.

August 4, 2021

The trajectory of marriage
will rise and fall
like the wavelike motion
of a woodpecker in flight,
like the ebb and flow
of the ocean
This is the natural evolution
Deal with regression
when it comes
Walk through the valleys
together

August 5, 2021

We were able to
remember,
rekindle,
rejuvenate,
reimagine,
reset,
reflect,
renew,
restore,
release,
receive

I was able to rediscover
my truest smile,
reconnect with
my spirited spirit,
realize that our marriage,
our love story
must be tended to
with as much loving care
as a young oak tree
Though it is resilient,
it needs to be nurtured

August 26, 2021

"We sense ourselves stir,
Slowly, sweetly,
As if for the first time.
This nearly tore us apart.
Yes, indeed.
It tears us to start."

-Amanda Gorman,
Call Us What We Carry

Happy 15 year Anniversary
In marriage
In education
In discovery
Happy 1st day of school
Another year of pandemic
teaching and leading
With my chest freshly stitched up
My mind scrubbed
from the viral devastation
My brain barely oxygenated
We start again

Are we ready?
Ready or not,
Here they come
Kids,
parents,
deadlines,
opinions,
expectations,
all the unknown,
the unspoken hurt,
the unprecedented loss,
not of learning,
but social emotional health

August 27, 2021

Who will step up
Build bridges towards healing
Who will step back
from the gaping hole,
Too afraid to fall in
Children do not need
extra hours to practice
letters and sounds
Teachers are fucking superheroes
and will help them in school,
in time

Children need time
to learn
how to play,
how to solve social problems,
how to grieve and work through
losing multiple family members,
how to regulate their immense emotions,
how to speak their hurt and ask for help,
how to listen,
how to be still,

Teachers require time
for those aforementioned needs as well

August 28, 2021

Still,
only slightly resilient
Aches and pains endured
My mask tight against my face
Lost in a sea of smiles
My DIY/PFIY (do it yourself/pay for it yourself)
heppa filter box fan
whirring in the background
I promised myself to
Not let stress eat me alive
Not be burdened by the news
Not spiral

Just face the light

August 29, 2021

And yet,
There is unpackaged trauma
Sitting before me
Sitting within me
Unfinished business
Unhappiness unmasked
Breathing these truths
Without speaking

And still,
No professionals to help
the traumatized teachers

And thus,
I teach and
I give and
I hug and
I love and
I read and
I heal

Everyday
Every way
I find my own way

Make your way towards
my lighthouse children
Let me be your beacon
Be your shield from the storm

September 1, 2021

My light is coming back
Yet the dark truth remains
Opinions and decisions
Put self before others
Health exemptions
Religious exemptions
Exempted from what?
Where is our responsibility to each other?
Angry parents
Banning mask mandates
COVID outbreaks
Unvaccinated colleagues and students
Unsafe work conditions

Teachers across America
flee in record numbers
Is anyone surprised?
The stress has taken its toll
It could've been me

How long will people
keep their heads
stuck in the sand?
How long can I continue
to fill from a leaking bucket?

September 21, 2021

I pledge allegiance to the teachers
Of the courageous countries
around the world
And to the student
For which he/she/they stand
One planet
Under love
Interconnected
With liberty and justice for all

October 10, 2021

Preparing for the race of a lifetime
Hours upon hours
Mile after silent mile
Changed
Charged
Ready
50k I'm on my way

And then
In a cruel twist of fate
just four days before race day
I contracted COVID 19

Are you serious Universe?
What the actual hell?
Mother Fucker!!!!!!
You knew this was a part of my healing
my journey of forgiveness and
back to self

I followed all the "rules"
This is not fair!
I cried for a hot moment
I sat on the toilet Googling
other ultramarathons around the country

I swore I would just run 50km
on my own
somewhere,
anywhere
in the woods
even though I couldn't
walk to the mailbox and back
without getting out of breath

I snapped out of it
so I could write a week's worth of sub plans

Seriously

And then
In the quiet of the quarantine
in between the naps and steam hits
after the fog lifted slightly
I realized the gift
that the Universe had presented me with

October 11, 2021

TIME

Time to write
and finally process all the trauma
No,
I would not toe the line
nor cross the finish
of my first ultramarathon
yet still,
somehow,
miraculously
I was transformed

During my perpetual
solitary confinement
I burst out of the cocoon
that had been suffocating me
for too long

And then,
well,
I let myself sit,
pumping rich oxygen into my veins
I began to let the words flow
I began to feel my spirit soar above me

October 12, 2021

Hindsight is 2020
Looking down,
looking back,
looking within,
I realized that the immense pressure
I had been under for so long,
had turned me into a diamond
The clear mind and
clear vision finally came

A dragonfly starts its life
in the darkness underwater
A monarch begins its transformation
in a suffocating chrysalis
A pearl is formed
as the result of a defense mechanism
deep in the sea
A diamond is created
under the earth's surface
after millions of years
and the perfect conditions
of heat and pressure

October 13, 2021

And what of myself?
I have finally allowed
the shitshow of a year,
the heat of the summer,
all of it,
to turn me into a
beautiful,
brilliant,
mother fucking jewel

I have allowed myself
to be honest with myself
and honest with my husband.
I have allowed myself
to be fully loved
by my longtime lover,
to accept the mud,
to breathe through the hard stuff,
and bloom fully

I reached out
in a time of true desperation
near rock bottom territory
and wholeheartedly allowed
the Universe to repair
a relationship worth saving

and also

help me return to the classroom
armed with invisible tools
to keep me grounded
and safe from mental destruction

October 14, 2021

With my newfound wings,
I am beginning to fly,
beginning to trust again,
continuing to grow and evolve,
continuing to teach what matters
no matter what,
to follow my dreams,
Absolutely loving
this crazy beautiful ride we're on
I am open and excited about all
that love has in store
Our love story
Etched in time,
yet ever unfolding

December 24, 2021

From the smoldering ashes
The Phoenix doth rise
So to has my spirit

Though the dark tried to
shroud my soul
I no longer fear it

Feel the love
pulsing from my heart
May you draw near it

I am limitless light embodied
Though the weight of the world
tried to crush
I have persevered it

I look up to the star studded skies
With enchanting emerald eyes
Graciously humble yet forever wise

From the lowest of lows
and highest of highs
Hear the roar of my
triumphant battle cries

Rise spirit rise

January 9, 2022

And still I hope,
I pray,
I believe
The Universe
will hear our calls
of desperate pleading
For collective healing

We are pieces of a whole
That long to be united
cradled and brought forth
through a
collective
magnificent
metamorphosis

BRIGHTER DAYS

_"We have the choice
to use the gift of our life
to make the world a better place -
or not to bother."_

-Dr. Jane Goodall

January 10, 2022

I interrupt the love waves
with another crash of reality
Globally, deaths from COVID
have reached over **5 million**

That's simply incomprehensible
Let us pause and remember
their lives which were cut short
Let us send healing love out
to their remaining loved ones.

January 11, 2022

Who needs a resolution?
What we need is a revolution.
A revelation
of everyday people
waking up
With purpose, passion, persistence

Knowing that it is our choice to make
How we choose to live our days
Our everyday existence
If you are blessed enough
to be reading this
Take heed

When you've hit rock bottom
And you feel you're all alone
Make a choice for yourself
For the world
To rise up

Find a way out of the abyss
Truly it is possible
The other side of sorrow is serenity
Just flip the coin

Flip your body towards the light
Look up

Flip your mind towards what you might
be able to do
if you let the warmth sink into your skin
Let the golden rays
Radiate through your pores and
Pour into the miraculously beating
heart of yours
Spread into every vein
and particle of your being

You are being called
to live your gift

January 15, 2022

The language of the soul is
Love
Art
Music
Thought
Revealing its
true colors,
true power,
true light
In dream form
In meditation
Sit with your soul awhile
Listen to what it has to say
Pay attention
Attend to your inner world
Connect to the divine within
Feel the cosmic connection
to all the divine in the Universe
Your soul is timeless,
genderless,
pure energy
Love embodied
Cut from the same cloth as all that is
It knows the longings of your heart
Long before you had words
to speak them into reality
Your soul is stirring the energy
that is the derivative of those dreams
Into a masterpiece in waiting

You are a dream star dragonfly
  Radiating with magnificent light
  Full of energy
  that will change the world
  Trust yourself
  Follow your heart

January 18, 2022

Words keep me alive
Encourage me to return
Day after day
Week after week
Month after month
Year after year

Encourage me to
show up,
rise up
Look for the pearl

These words were gifted to me
During my preservice teaching days
From a wise and wonderful professor
They have become my go to mantra

My lifesaver,
my lighthouse,
my question of the day
To all my students

Here's the truth about a natural
pearl in the wild
Something irritating
enters an oyster or clam or the like
As a defense, that mollusk secretes
layer after layer of fluid

Day after day
Week after week
Month after month
Year after year
to cover the
Pain of a grain

And 1 in 10,000 chances
A beautiful lustrous pearl is formed
From irritating to illuminating
A gem is born

And so it is our often arduous task
In the everyday grind
To find
Our own pearls
To see how the pain
of the past few years
Has formed us all into
Magnificent clairvoyant crystals

If it's still not clear
Be patient
Know that your oyster
Your soul
Is working over time
In its own time
To make the mess that its in
A brilliant work of art
Something worth admiring
remembering

January 23, 2022

Here are just a few pearls from my
2020 gratitude journal
Words that lifted me up
Offering a breeze beneath my torn wings
Thank God I had the wherewithal
to write a snippet of hope
at the end of each day
These flickers of light
provided just enough fuel
to keep me burning

Mrs. Ziegler, you look like
an inside out watermelon.
I love the beautiful blue sky.
I feel confident to speak up
and change the world.
Mom, Kate is so cute.
I'm glad God gave her to us.
I am. I can. I will.
Weeeee. This is fun. Again. Again.
I love you. Never retire.
Do you believe in fairies?
Emma, listen, I just want to be a grape.
She's the type of person
you just need to flow with the river with.
Sharing is caring.
Turn on the rock and roll!
What the chickens?
This was the best day of our lives.

Mrs. Ziegler, you're a hero.
I feel happy and strong.
God gives the best hugs
even though he lives in our hearts.
How do goats mate?
Why was Emma born first?
What does digest mean?
How do you spell Gitche Gumee?
Just a little snuggle.
Take a breath.
No doubt, I have the best family ever.
Yeah mom, fight!
It's okay to be different.
You're precious.
Mom, sit down and watch my moves.
I see an angel.
I NEED TOILET PAPER!!!
More passion.
Mrs. Ziegler, how do you stay so beautiful?
I am not giving up.
I just want to sit with you.
Help the little ones write their books.
If I had to pick the best teacher
out of the whole entire world
I would choose you!

January 24, 2022

Take your sufferings
Cast them to the wind
Plug into YOUR power source
In order to have the energy
To
dare I say
SHINE YOUR LIGHT
Throughout the world

January 25, 2022

The certainty of hope
Is that it's always available
Even in the never ending
uncertain times
In every situation

The power of hope is real
And is a source of strength
In the everyday struggle to survive

Activate hope
Activate your light
Take a leap towards your vision
Live by the light of compassion
Calm clarity is yours to embrace

Ignite the spark of hope
Now
Infinitely
Change
Renew

Reignite when hope is lost
We can
We must

January 26, 2022

It's a miracle
How a single ray of sunshine
Can cut through the darkness
As it stretches out across the sky
One beam of golden light
Fans out in a heavenly arch
Creating clouds of every color
Piercing the soul
Washing away worries
Leaving nothing but
Peace
It's a miracle
How sitting with the rising sun
Can provide so much hope
As the Earth spins
And the world turns from dark to light

Be brave
Rise up
Shine your light

It's a miracle
To be alive
Celebrate that simple yet profound truth
And make the most
Out of the gift of today

February 2, 2022

From Clarity to clusterfuck
We lived through darkness,
raging storms,
unease beyond compare

Easy for us to say
Those blessed to live another day

Exhaustion set in
Our bones and souls despaired
Would we live to see our dreams
Set in to motion

We thought
Something's gotta give
And either it did
Or it will
Thy will be done

All we know is
we're done with hate
Done with ignorance
and mistreatment of
fellow humans,
fellow planetary life
And ready for love to rule

For love is
    And was
    And will be
    forever and ever

    And so
    our spirits carry on with the
    Phoenix rising
    Towards brighter days
    A better place
    For all

NOTES

———————————————

*"A bird doesn't sing
because it has an answer,
it sings because it has a song."*

– Maya Angelou

On February 14, 2022,
just weeks after my last journal entry,
I was sent another test.
another threat made directly towards me.
However, this time,
a new crew of misinformed bullies
were not as emboldened
to knock down my door
with oppressive, uneducated,
ignorant, fearful words.
First they emailed,
then they called,
then they spoke my name
at a school board meeting.
Turns out, this group of people
was so radically opposed
to my use of inclusive literature
in the classroom
that they wanted me "disciplined"
and fired.

Would I let love rule?
Or would darkness prevail?
I'll tell you what won...LOVE!
Fortunately, I was supported
by those that mattered,
and the homophobic hate speech
was
shut
down.

Unfortunately, this type of action
against teachers and public education
is happening all over the country
and is causing
a mass exodus of educators.
So on top of the teacher shortages
that already exist for their own reasons,
we now have expert educators
leaving the field
due to systemic issues
causing severe stress (to put it lightly).

During this time,
people reached out to me
apologizing that I was having
to deal with such nonsense,
feeling sorry for me,
asking if I was okay.
All I could do was laugh.

The truth is,
their actions made me feel
so proud of myself.
I'm glad those bullies
spoke my name to the public,
for then it would be recorded in history
what I stood for.
Love and justice for all.
Common sense.

I would not and will not ever let
that type of behavior
scare me or stop me
from doing what is right,
for the sake of all the children,
especially those whose voices
are silenced and whose human rights
are being stripped away.

I will continue to rock the boat,
shine a light on injustices,
and speak up when needed.
I've learned throughout this
global pandemic
that I'm a lot stronger
than I give myself credit for.
I believe the educational system
is stronger than the stories of injustices
happening today.

As Dr. Susan Murray,
of the Royal College of Surgeons
in Dublin states,
"If we are not prepared
fight fear and ignorance
as actively and as thoughtfully
as we fight any other virus,
it is possible that fear
can do terrible harm
to vulnerable people."

And so fight I will.
We must all stay vigilant.
Those bullies will be back.
They'll run for boards.
They'll try to get their way.
But there is no place for hate.
Love always wins!
The truth seekers
who will do whatever it takes
to make ALL students feel
seen, heard, and welcome –
that's who will win!

I raise my hands to the sky
And offer my eternal gratitude
I return to my heart
Close my eyes
Wrapped in extraordinary peace

This work of poetry
and mindful musings
was a sorrowful song to write.
Words often failed to reflect
the clouded mirror of my mind
that was so often shrouded in pain,
carrying the trauma of my students,
the trauma of a country,
the trauma/gift of leading
the most challenging class
I've ever taught
through a global pandemic

All I wanted was to return to center.
I couldn't. I simply could not.
Colors faded. Spirit trapped.
Joy nearly extinguished.

Thankfully, I'm now able to look
at the sad words on the page
like the notes of a despairing melody.
Just as your favorite ballad
or hymn stirs you to tears
yet leaves you filled,
this song stirred something in me
and left me healed.

> *"Let's not forget these early days*
> *Remember we begin the same*
> *We lose our way in fear and pain*
> *Oh joy begin."*
> -Dave Matthews

Like a bird,
I don't have all the answers,
but my song had to be sung.
Like the tree spirit told me in California,
I had to sing my song
for the world to hear.

Let joy in!

We have lived through,
and in some cases,
are still living through
extremely difficult times.
Whatever situation
you find yourself in,
know that it's only temporary.
You're allowed to feel all the feelings.
To grieve.
To cry.
To scream and kick and yell.

But then you must
find a way forward.
You must step outside
your body and mind
and not let your emotions
eat you alive.
You must not let
whatever mountains you're climbing
stop you from becoming
best version of you.

You can hope for better days.
Then, you must act.

Life is so much better
when we give and receive love
with reckless abandon.
Life is far more meaningful
when we take time
to notice and give thanks
for all the small things,
all the miracles,
all the helpers who have our back.

I hope my teacher
in the trenches story
and our love story
reminds you that while
life, love, and teaching
are messy and hard and chaotic,
they can also be blissful,
full of light,
and absolutely extraordinary.

ACKNOWLEDGEMENTS

Dear reader, thank you for coming along with me on that journey. It was only a tad painful, right? I appreciate you taking time out of your busy, brilliant, beautiful life to read my words. I hope it will help you continue to spread your light.

I'd like to take a moment here to honor all the amazing teachers that I worked alongside for 15 years before and socially distanced from during the hardest damn year and a half of my life. To my Forest Park family, I appreciate all of you. Your dedication, tenacity, resilience, and creativity were heroic. Never forget the influence you have on those in your presence.

Of all the incredible educator heroes out there, I'd like to thank a few that really had my back and my heart through the darkest of days. To Lauri Patterson,

Allison Soderberg, Kayla Peterson, Debi Bendick, Benjamin Haight...I don't think I could've done it without you. You deserve a golden apple teacher award (and maybe a million dollar raise)!

Next, I need to thank all the angels out in California that came to our immediate rescue. God was truly working overtime during our trip out west and the presence of the Holy Spirit could be felt as tangible as my toes in the sand. Of course there were others back home that held us in prayer as well. For them, we give unending thanks. Each of the following helpers was hand picked by the Universe to be exactly where it was at the exact moment we needed it.

To Tracy, the facial/massage therapist from Sonoma. Erich surprised me by booking an hour session with this beautiful angel. It was an absolute blessing to be in her space with the perfect essential oils swirling through the air, crystals sparkling in the corners, and completely calming energy filling the space. As she was caressing my face, massaging my shoulders, working miracles of all kinds, Tracy asked, "Do you do a lot of body work? Your body responds so well to it." I wish! The last massage I got was during my sister's bachelorette party weekend. I told her briefly about who I was, where we were from, our life with three girls, what marriage was like after fifteen years. "Girl, you are in it!" She understood. She also told me to spend thirty minutes a day meditating on my dreams.

To Lindsay, the owner and mastermind designer of the Zen Jewel Sanctuary VRBO. The cottage, the magical garden, the space, the CDs, the books, the energy, all of it was so incredibly healing. This is where we got into everything and returned to one another.

To The Ocean, oh the ebbs and flows of your water, moving in rhythm with the moon, pulling on my emotions. The turquoise blue green waves that crash mightily, sending ripples of wind through my hair. Your healing breath. The salt that sustains so much life and keeps me afloat.

To The Eagle, the spirit animal that showed up in multiple places, sending us messages from the Universe. On our last morning at the Zen Jewel, Erich and I went for a run along the ocean to offer our dozen roses as a gift to the sea. The surprise anniversary bouquet was a sweet gift from Tracy the massage therapist from Sonoma. I knew they wouldn't make our entire two week journey and seeing that we had just spent two days rediscovering our love and rekindling our relationship, we decided this was the perfect way to part with the flowers. As we crossed the rolling sand dunes to head to shore, there was a bald eagle. It took to the sky in all its majesty. We ceremoniously threw the roses into the ocean, giving thanks to each other and this place. It had been nothing short of transformational. It should come as no surprise that I brought along my Book of Beasties by Sarah Seidelmann on this trip, so as soon as we got back from our run, I opened it up to read more about Eagle's message. "Eagles are astonishingly loyal and will stay in partnerships for decades. You are being asked by Eagle to set your differences aside and join forces with an intimate partner...and you'll want to be lenient with your chosen partners, too." I cried. How did I almost walk away from this partnership, from my person that has been so loyal. Erich was definitely channeling Eagle's energy when he said to me earlier on the old green couch, "You don't have to apologize about your feelings from the past." We each have been learning how to be more lenient and grow in our partnership.

To Ron Hanson, the 83 year old who had been married to his wife of 65 years that we met in Founders Cove on the Avenue of the Giants. He was a teacher for thirteen years, then a missionary in Kenya and Tanzania for forty. We talked for a good five minutes about love. He told us the secret of marriage was each giving 100% and having Jesus in your hearts. He prayed for us. We walked away holding hands and giggling. I told Erich I wished I could've recorded the whole conversation. Guess what? I accidentally did! I had no idea. Thanks Universe.

To Marco, the spicy caretaker of the Golden Eagle VRBO in Trinidad. When I asked him if love was a decision or a choice, he said, "Love is blind." You see, after marrying his wife, the woman who rescued him from a life of living on the streets of LA, and coming out as bisexual (something he thought she already knew about him), she stayed with him and they've been married for 35 years. Despite his mother in law hating him, despite the ridicule from the Catholic church, despite nearly getting killed by a runaway murderer (yeah, his stories were insane), their love remains strong. The secret of marriage, according to Marco, was "communication, and a little fight to keep things steamy!" He brought us a gigantic bottle of tequila and lit our bonfire with a torch when he found out we were celebrating our fifteenth anniversary. What an angelic character he was. And what a steamy evening we had.

To The Otters, the fabulously designed statues in various locations up and down the coast to bring awareness to protecting local watersheds. Thank you for returning my awareness to how much I love falling asleep holding hands with my lover, just as you hold paws while you sleep so you don't drift apart.

To The Seals, I don't know. There was just something about them. Like they were barking and clapping and cheering us on.

To the stranger at Wedding Rock who asked, "Did you put a ring on it?" To which we replied, "fifteen years ago. Just renewing our vows." "Right on!" Cue the Californian thumb and pinky fist shake.

To the bartender and patrons at the Port o' Pints in Crescent City, where we were introduced to the song, "On a Beach in Hawaii," which I have since renamed Erich's mating call.

To Gineen, the spunky waitress at the Hiochi Cafe who gave us directions to her favorite skinny dipping hole. She'd been married for 54 years. Her secret to marriage...tolerance. And might I add, confidence and fun and spontaneity! She said she skinny dipped at this hole at least once a year with her husband. Erich and I hiked to the hot spot, but it was a bit too crowded to strip off our clothes and jump in together. Someday.

To Y'n, a kind man from Iowa who we first met along with his wife and two kids at a Thai restaurant in northern California. He offered love advice, laughter, and instant connection. We ended up seeing each other again on our flight home. We were in line behind them in the terminal. Erich and I looked at each other. No way! YES WAY!!! He turned around. Said our names, and gave us both a big hug. We continued our conversation about life and love and marriage. What a fun surprise.

To Steve and Molly, the owners of the Point Reyes Vineyard that we stayed at for a night. A beautiful couple who has been through it all and even more lovely as a result of all their struggle.

And now to others close to home that were there and continue to be there to listen, to encourage, to hold me, to make me laugh, to offer positive healing energy, to remind me of the incredible grace of God and help me let go of guilt and shame. Amanda and DJ Rasner, friends and colleagues who wrote incredible letters of support, Gina Onderak, Barb Luck, Adrienne Newman, Stacy Wonfor, Kristen Peterson, my Tenergy Breathe for Change friends, my amazing sister - I don't even know where to start - I thank God that you're in my life, my soul sisters. Thank you for helping me move forward. I love you all so so much.

To my extraordinarily talented and beautiful friend and artist, Melanie Bess. You were there to help me through the hot mess I was in and were the perfect one to capture the essence of it all in the book cover. Thank you for pushing me, believing in me, and dreaming big dreams! I appreciate you beyond words.

I could write a whole book about the next person I need to thank. My mother. You have been there for me through all the ups and downs and I haven't always treated you the best. In regards to this story, I just have to say, you were right all along...about everything. I am sorry for the pain I caused and the sleepless nights you suffered through as a result. You were already dealing with the physical pain of a knee replacement and your own pandemic mental strain and then you had to dive into the depths of hell I found myself in...because that's what mothers do. I read somewhere recently that the inability to receive support is a trauma response. That makes perfect sense. As much as you tried, I was truly incapable of hearing your words, heeding your advice, forgiving and loving again. Teaching through the pandemic and crawling through a traumatic school year left me like a withered grape vine. I am sorry. From the bottom of my heart, I thank you. I love you.

To my family as a whole, all of you, thank you for your constant love and support. You kept me grounded during the uncertain times. Knowing I always have you to catch me when I fall makes going through hard times and going out on a limb a bit easier.

To our why, our girls...if and when you ever read this, I'm sorry for losing my temper from time to time, I'm sorry for any pain I may have caused you. Know that I was always just trying to do my best juggling it all. I hope this has provided just a morsel of guidance in the world of love, marriage, and life. It's not perfect. It's not always pretty and pearly. But it's still all so worth it. Thank you for giving your dad and I so much to be thankful for every second of every day. You make us laugh, challenge us to be better, give us so much hope and joy. We are so unbelievably proud of all of you. I love you from the depths of the earth to the ever expanding corners of the Universe and back...forever and ever.

Lastly, to my husband, my partner for life. We've said it all, so I'll keep it short and sweet...I'm sorry. I love you. Endlessly. Thank you for always believing in me, in us.

ABOUT THE AUTHOR

Chandra Ziegler is a mother, teacher, literacy coach, certified yoga instructor, silent sport enthusiast, dreamer extraordinaire, and light spreader. Chandra is the author of *Extraordinary Endurance: A Training Plan for the Marathon of Life* and *Let Nature Be Your Teacher*. She lives in the beautiful Upper Peninsula of Michigan with her husband, three daughters, and two black labs. Follow her on Facebook, Instagram @chandra_z or at www.dreamstardragonfly.com.